iScience

Insects:
Which One Doesn't Belong?

by Emily Sohn and Karen J. Rothbardt

Chief Content Consultant
Edward Rock
Associate Executive Director, National Science Teachers Association

NORWOOD HOUSE PRESS
Chicago, IL

Norwood House Press
PO Box 316598
Chicago, IL 60631

For information regarding Norwood House Press, please visit our website at
www.norwoodhousepress.com or call 866-565-2900.

Special thanks to: Amanda Jones, Amy Karasick, Alanna Mertens and Terrence Young, Jr.

Editors: Jessica McCulloch, Barbara Foster, Diane Hinckley
Designer: Daniel M. Greene
Production Management: Victory Productions, Inc.

Library of Congress Cataloging-in-Publication Data

Sohn, Emily.

Insects : which one doesn't belong? / by Emily Sohn and Karen J. Rothbardt.
p. cm.—(iScience readers)

Summary: "Describes what makes an insect an insect and teaches traits
by which readers can recognize them. As readers use scientific inquiry to
learn how different insects grow and change, an activity based on real world
situations challenges them to apply what they've learned in order to solve a
puzzle"—Provided by publisher.

Includes bibliographical references and indexes.

ISBN-13: 978-1-59953-407-7 (library edition: alk. paper)
ISBN-10: 1-59953-407-X (library edition: alk. paper)

1. Insects—Juvenile literature. I. Rothbardt, Karen. II. Title.

QL467.2.S64 2012
595.7—dc22
2011011534

Manufactured in the United States of America in North Mankato, Minnesota.

175N—072011

Contents

iScience Puzzle   6

Discover Activity   8

Things in Common   9

Connecting to History   14

Science at Work   16

Growing Up   17

Solve the iScience Puzzle   20

Beyond the Puzzle   21

Glossary   22

Further Reading/Additional Notes   23

Index   24

Note to Caregivers:

Throughout this book, many questions are posed to the reader. Some are open-ended and ask what the reader thinks. Discuss these questions with your child and guide him or her in thinking through the possible answers and outcomes. There are also questions posed which have a specific answer. Encourage your child to read through the text to determine the correct answer. Most importantly, encourage answers grounded in reality while also allowing imaginations to soar. Information to help support you as you share the book with your child is provided in the back in the **Additional Notes** section.

Words that are **bolded** are defined in the glossary in the back of the book.

In the Buzz

Have you ever seen a giraffe in your home? Chances are, the answer is no. But you've likely seen an insect in your home. Think of two animal lists: "Insects" and "Everything Else." The "Insect" list is longer!

In this book, you will learn lots of facts about insects.

great green bush cricket

Which One Does Not Belong?

More than a million kinds of insects live on Earth.

Look at these pictures.

Three of the creatures are insects. One creature is not an insect.

Option 1: Mosquito

Option 2: Centipede

Option 3: Ant

6

Option 4: Ladybug

What do all the creatures have in common?

What makes them different?

Which creature does not belong?

All of these creatures are insects. Can you name one thing they all have in common?

Discover Activity

Finding Insects

Look through magazines and newspapers. Search for animals. (Hint: *National Geographic* and other science magazines are good places to start.) First, ask an adult if it's okay. Then, cut out the pictures. Which do you think are insects?

Materials

- old newspapers and science magazines
- glue
- poster board
- scissors

There could be lots of pictures of insects in these old newspapers and magazines.

Now, group the pictures. You could arrange them by size or by color. What other groups can you think of? Glue your pictures onto a poster board. Name as many animals as you can.

Things in Common

Every insect has six legs and two antennae. Can you find those parts on this bee?

Here's how all insects are alike.

All of the adults have a head and a body. They also have six legs.

On their heads are two skinny stick-like parts. These are called **antennae.**

Go back to the iScience Puzzle pictures. Can you find a head in each picture?

Body Parts

Look at the body of an adult insect. It has three sections. These are **segments.**

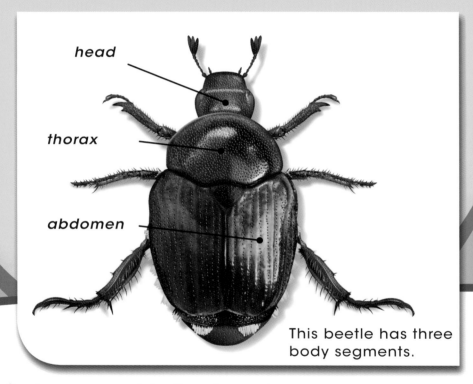

head

thorax

abdomen

This beetle has three body segments.

The first segment is the head.

The second is the **thorax.**

The third is the **abdomen.**

Can you see which iScience Puzzle choices have three segments?

Structure

Your bones are under your skin. But insects are not like us. Their **skeletons** are on the outside. Their skeletons are like shells.

This cicada grew a new skeleton and crawled out of the old one. It's sort of like you wearing bigger clothes as you grow.

old skeleton

When an insect grows, it **molts.** The old skeleton falls off. Then the insect grows a new one.

Which iScience Puzzle choices look like they have skeletons on the outside?

Little Sniffers

Insects do not have noses. But they can still smell.

Antennae give them sniff powers. All insects have two antennae. Their sniffers, on the antennae, come in many shapes. Some are big. Some are small.

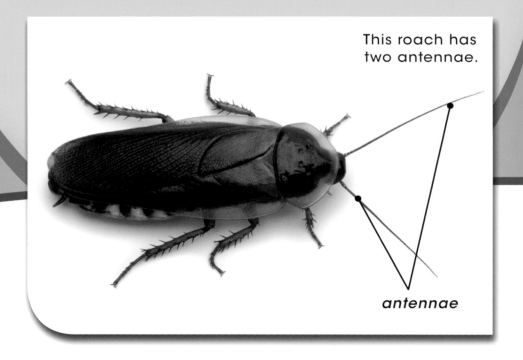

This roach has two antennae.

antennae

Look at the iScience Puzzle creatures. Which ones have antennae?

Do You See What I See?

Insects use eyes to see. Some insects look like they have two eyes. But each eye is made of lots of tiny eyes. You need a microscope to see them. These are called **compound eyes.** They can see forward, backward, up, down, and sideways all at the same time!

Each section of a horsefly's eye is like a tiny eye all by itself.

horsefly eye, shown bigger than in real life

eyes

Look at the iScience Puzzle photos. Can you find eyes on the creatures? How many eyes do you see on each?

The silk thread is dyed and wound on spools. The thread will be woven into fabric.

cocoons

silkworm

Connecting to History

Making Silk

Silk is soft, smooth, and beautiful. Best of all, insects can help make it. People in China learned to make silk thousands of years ago. Their secret helpers? Silkworms.

These insects are not really worms. They are more like caterpillars. They are moth **larvae.**

Silkworms make silk threads. They use the threads to spin their cocoons. To get the threads, people unwound the cocoons. Then they used the threads to make fabric.

Today, people still make silk this way.

Madagascar hissing cockroach on a grownup's hand

Did You Know?

Insects may be small. But some make a lot of noise!

Most insects rub their legs together to make noise. The Madagascar cockroach does something else. It pushes air through holes in its body. That makes a sound that goes "Hisssss."

Some insect sounds are friendly. They attract other insects of the same kind. Other sounds are angry and mean! They scare away creatures that want to eat the insects.

Science at Work

Entomologist

Some kids love to catch insects. Some adults do it for a living.

Entomologists study insects. They are scientists. Entomologists spend lots of time outside. They look for new kinds of insects that don't have names yet. They watch how insects act. And they collect insects to study. There is still so much to learn about insects!

Insects are a key part of nature. If you collect them, put them back where you found them. And ask an adult first. Some insects can bite and sting. And some cause allergies.

Also, be gentle. Insects are smaller than you!

TAILED JAY
Graphium agamemnon

Catopsilia Pomona

BLUE BOTTLE
Graphium sarpedon

These butterflies appear to be grouped by size. Can you think of another way to group them?

STRIPED BLUE CROW
Euploea mulciber

RED HELEN
Papilio helenus

BANDED JEZEBEL
Delias descombesi

16

Growing Up

This katydid is laying eggs.

Insects have mothers and fathers. Parents mate. Then a mother insect lays eggs.

The eggs **hatch.** Baby insects grow into adults.

The adults lay eggs. Eventually the adults die.

This is called a life cycle. It keeps going and going.

Butterfly Cycle

As you grow, you change. But you still look like you. Some insects are another story. Take butterflies. Young ones don't look like adults at all.

When their eggs hatch, caterpillars come out. These are the larvae. After a few weeks, each larva makes a covering for itself. It is now a **pupa.**

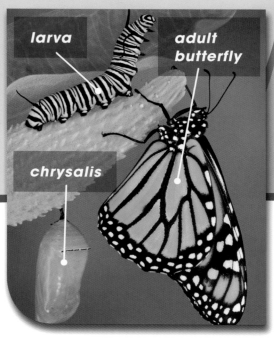

larva

adult butterfly

chrysalis

It may be hard to believe. But a caterpillar and a butterfly are two forms of the same animal!

The covering is like a cocoon. It is called a **chrysalis.**

Weeks later, the pupa has changed. A butterfly comes out. The change is called **metamorphosis.**

One in a Million

Not all insects build cocoons or chrysalises. But many change a lot as they grow.

Take grasshoppers. Their eggs hatch into **nymphs.** They look almost like little adults. But nymphs have no wings. They lose their skin many times. This is called molting. As adults, they can walk, hop, and fly.

Is this grasshopper a nymph or an adult? How can you tell?

Other insects just grow as they age. They look the same, just bigger.

Do you change like a grasshopper as you age? Or will you look the same, just bigger? Think ahead five years. Now think about 20 years from now. Do you think you will be able to do anything then that you can't do now?

Solve the ⓘScience Puzzle

Now use what you learned in the book to solve the puzzle.

Option 1: Mosquito

Option 2: Centipede

Option 3: Ant

Option 4: Ladybug

Which creature does not have six legs?

Which creature does not have three parts to its body?

(Hint: Insects aren't the only animals with antennae or skeletons on the outside of their bodies.)

That's right! The centipede is not an insect.

Beyond the Puzzle

You learned a lot about insects. Look back at your poster board. Which pictures are insects? Have you changed any answers?

Now, go out on a walk. Bring a pencil and paper. Look for small creatures. When you find one, draw it.

At home, look at your drawings. Are they insects? Quiz your family and friends. Then explain your answers.

There are so many insects in the world. You can try to find a new one every time you go for a walk!

How can this boy tell if the creature on his face is an insect or not?

Glossary

abdomen: the third segment of an insect.

antennae: thin structures on an insect's head that the insect uses to smell and feel things.

chrysalis: a hard shell that protects a pupa as it turns into a butterfly.

compound eyes: many little simple eyes in one big eye.

entomologists: scientists who study insects.

hatch: to come out of an egg.

larvae: wingless, worm-shaped forms of insects that come out of eggs.

metamorphosis: a change in form that happens during development.

molts: sheds an outer shell.

nymphs: young forms of insects such as grasshoppers.

pupa: the stage between a larva and an adult.

segments: parts or sections of an insect's body.

silk: thread or fabric made from silkworm fibers.

skeletons: hard parts of an animal's body.

thorax: the middle section of an insect.

Further Reading

Insects & Spiders, by Noel Tait. Simon & Schuster Children's Publishing, 2008.

National Wildlife Federation Field Guide to Insects and Spiders of North America, by Arthur V. Evans. Sterling Publishing, 2007.

The Insects Home Page. http://www.earthlife.net/insects/six.html

Bugs, Bug Pictures, Insects— National Geographic. http://animals.nationalgeographic.com/animals/bugs/

Additional Notes

The page references below provide answers to questions asked throughout the book. Questions whose answers will vary are not addressed.

Page 7: Caption question: They all have six legs.

Page 11: They all have skeletons on the outside. Some creatures that are not insects also have skeletons on the outside.

Page 12: They all have antennae. Some creatures that are not insects also have antennae.

Page 19: Caption questions: An adult. You can tell because it has wings.

Page 21: Caption question: An insect has antennae, six legs, and a three-part body (head, thorax, and abdomen).

Index

abdomen, 10

antennae, 9, 12

butterfly, 18

butterfly collection, 16

caterpillar, 14, 18

centipede, 6, 20

chrysalis, 18

cocoon, 14, 18

compound eyes, 13

eggs, 17–19

entomologist, 16

grasshopper, 19

head, 9–10

larva, 14, 18

legs, 9, 20

life cycle, 17

Madagascar hissing
  cockroach, 15

metamorphosis, 18

molt, 11, 19

moth, 14

nymph, 19

pupa, 18

segments, 10

silk, 14

silkworm, 14

skeleton, 11

thorax, 10